Acknowledgment

Revelation 12:11

Introduction

LINDA D. LEE

*"You must learn to master
a new way to think
before you can master
a new way to be."*
- Marianne Williamson

VEIL
Verb: cover with or as though with a veil
Synonyms: envelop, surround, swathe, enfold, cover, conceal, hide, screen, shield, cloak, blanket, shroud; obscure.

TRANSITIONING
Verb: gerund or present participle: transitioning
Undergo or cause to undergo a process or period of transition.

MINDSET
Noun: The established set of attitudes held by someone.

- Merriam-Webster Dictionary

For this project, *Lifting the Veil: Transitioning from a Ministry to Business Mindset,* it is critical to begin with definitions. I want you to understand what you will have to endure on this journey. When the Holy Spirit begun to transition me into a Kingdompreneur, I did not have a clue what I was doing. A friend had just introduced me to Periscope so that I could listen to their sermons. And laughing, I thought I was really doing something by using Facebook. Little did I know, I had already sabotaged, unbeknown to me, someone's scope because I was ignorant of social media business etiquette. Frankly speaking, I was still operating with a ministry mindset and had become judgmental of a Kingdompreneur's content because scoping was unusual to me.

You have made the best investment of your life. Many emerging entrepreneurs have a desire to help people but do not know where to begin. For the past eight years all I have known is ministry. Which is not a bad thing. But a paradigm shift was taking place.

Webster defines paradigm shift as a fundamental change in approach or underlying assumptions. God was transitioning my ministry into a business during this shift. The first step had to take place in my mind. My mindset needed to change to align with what God was doing. To some people, this may have been a transition, but for me it was a little more difficult. My Kingdompreneurship is in its third year. The first two years I focused on social media etiquette and learning.

A mentor suggested a list of business courses to me while I was receiving a theology degree and perfecting (maturing) my skills as a Family Relationship Midwife ®. I took some courses like: Passion Plan, Release Your Vision, How to Become An Irresistible International Speaker, Identify Circle of Influence, Goal Setting, Time Management, Business Plan Writing, Leading an Organization, Building a Successful Team, Success Blueprint, Facebook for Business, How to Become Extremely Successful, Marketing Strategies, Jump Start Your Thinking, 21 Days to Build an Solid Brand, Entrepreneur Spirit Mastermind Class Traits of Storytelling, Branding, LinkedIn for Business, Powerful Presentations, Effective Communication, Utilizing a Virtual Business, Intellectual Property, Cross-Cultural Competency Training Passport Program, and International Standards, just to name a few. While others were doing extra-curricular activities, I sacrificed that time to transition my mindset. You will need to do something similar: Sacrifice your time to learn.

When it comes to Kingdompreneurship, you must possess a combination of theology, business foundation, and principles for each one. There are competencies in business that you will need, and you will need to be a living epistle while God expands your territory. Do not fool yourself: it will not happen overnight. Be patient.

"And they overcame him by the blood of the Lamb
And *by the word of their testimony,*
And they did not love their lives to the death."
-Revelation 12:11

Get ready to read four proven strategies from entrepreneurs trying to transition from a ministry mindset to a business mindset. These powerhouse stories will teach you leadership qualities concealed within each word. It will be up to you to discern the strategy God released in the life of each entrepreneur.

When building a successful business, there are a few things you must do:

- Mentally prepare for a leadership role
- Develop and strengthen your leadership skills
- Be prepared to invest in your business growth, visibility and creditability

The first step in becoming a Kingdompreneur is getting a changed mindset. Now enjoy the resilience and endurance of some phenomenal women.

CHAPTER 2

Was Blind, But Now I See!

LORETTA HOWARD

"Make a joyful shout to the LORD, all you lands!"
- Psalm 100:1

With the diagnosis of a degenerative eye disease, a job lay off, a 30k pay cut, a mortgage and the death of my parents in my late twenties, it seemed that STRUGGLE was my middle name and grief was my good, better and best friend.

It was as if my life puzzle slipped out of my hands and shattered so forcefully that the pieces could never lock securely in place again.

"Lord, how do I live without my Mama!" I will never to be able to give her a secure smile and say I love him. "She will never see me get married!" "I will never be able to introduce her to my children." I had always dreamed of giving her my child and telling her what eye color they had. Emotionally ripped apart, I declined a marriage proposal because I did not want to get married in such a broken emotional state.

Time, prayers and tears allowed me to begin, halt, and begin the grief process over and over. I just personally yearned to know if the hurt would ever end. Never fully understanding, I just needed to LET IT GO!

Jesus simply carried me - this blob of a person with a shattered spirit, every day through the day homework - home with so many tears. It was as if I was in an alternate dimension of my own life. As Jesus carried me, I could see glimpses of happiness - I just could not get there. I would pray at the altar at church and it was as if I would give the grief to God, but the human hurt made me take the grief back.

Finally, I gave it all to HIM, and He took the two years' grief and made me aware that I had an abundant life to live. The pay cut - He simply breathed on my finances. It never added up, but He provided. The eye disease lead to multiple surgeries, but I stood strong and in the knowledge of His promises. He truly never FAILS—what a wonderful Father He is!

Psalm 100:1

Was Blind, But Now I See! Exercise

Blindness can be natural or spiritual. For you to transition from a ministry to a business mindset, you must establish other sets of attributes. You must identify areas that need to be shifted but not necessarily changed, because with God all things are possible. Loretta experienced one traumatic experience after another. God removed people and items precious to her, while strengthening her spiritual sight. A veil was being lifted and Kingdompreneurship was birthing inside her. She finally yielded her will and surrendered to God's will. He laid the foundation for a non-profit called Mrs. Lottie's Pantry in memory of her mother, Mrs. Lottie Smith Howard. Annotate blind areas in your life that need a mindset shift:

_____

_____

_____

_____

CHAPTER 3

Restored to Sanity
OLLYN YVONNE ADKINS

*"Commit your works to the LORD;
And your thoughts will be established."*
- Proverbs 16:3

Spiritual silence. I fell to the floor in the family room of our home. I could hear my 12-year-old son screaming for help, instructing his younger sister to call 911. He yelled for help, and with his fist he beat my chest yelling, "MOMMA NO!" I could hear but not respond.

Another overdose, opiate addiction. This time the kids saw it all. There was no more hiding. The pain pills had full control of my life. Every thought, every action, every minute of the day. After several years of treatment for a back injury, I found my life spiraling out of control. Detoxification treatment centers and promises to never do this again. All lies. Every good intention always ended up being a lie, and self-will was not enough. Several years after this incident, facing the loss of my marriage, my home, my children, my soul. Tired of lying, manipulating, pleading, borrowing, stealing. I checked into a local drug treatment center with a made-up mind. I was introduced to narcotics anonymous groups, and there my healing began. After following simple directions, sponsorship and completing the 12 steps of Narcotics Anonymous, my life became manageable. I came to understand God. I also found that the darkness had been overcome. Reflecting the content of the literature "more will be revealed." I had been restored to sanity.

    I had a "spiritual awakening." God revealed His plan for the addict for those who would accept His son Jesus, forsaking all other gods. The illumination of a spiritual revelation was born; Recovery Room Ministries. A Christ-Centered ministry and curriculum developed to aid in the restoration of the hurting to a life of hope, love, deliverance, sanctification and stability. My life's purpose is to be a light and a vessel offering God's plan to all God's people.

Proverbs 16:3

Restored to Sanity Exercise

Overcoming addiction or mental bondage is a process. As Ollyn shared, she had to be broken: "Every good intention always ended up being a lie, and self-will was not enough. Several years after this incident, facing the loss of my marriage, my home, my children, my soul. Tired of lying, manipulating, pleading, borrowing, stealing...," positioned her for a new mindset. Are you ready to move from insane to sanity? Are you tired of being sick and tired? Are you ready to live and not just exist? Are you tired of being in the same place you were last year? Annotate blind areas in your life that you need a mindset shift regarding:

_____

_____

_____

_____

_____

CHAPTER 4

Never Give Up!
PEACE UCHE

"For the Lord is good; His mercy is everlasting. And His truth endures to all generations."
- Psalm 100:5

Your ability to shell yourself from problems and come out of it still loving, caring, trusting, humble, respectful and hopeful is what makes you forever young.

After high school, it took me four years to get into a higher institution to study nursing, and when I got in, I experienced an emotional roller coaster that strengthened and taught me that nobody but God has got your back. Even when I felt like God left me, I could not afford to not depend on Him. I am a nurse; initially I had my reasons for working in a school, while not knowing that God had another reason for me to be there. He wanted me to discover the need to stop this barbaric practice called female genital mutilation by getting the students to be involved in planning and organizing awareness campaigns against this practice that had been a menace to female children across the globe, with the aim to eradicate the practice by the next generation. Be sensitive to know when God is calling your attention to a need.

Thanks to Mr. Bamigbose (An Economist at Debiruss College) and Linda D Lee, I was encouraged to actualize this vision no matter how it turned out. To the glory of God, the first campaign I launched at Debiruss College was a success, and all doubts and pessimism were eventually buried.

Now I am the founder of a Nongovernmental Organization (NGO) called The Vrede Marte Foundation that will carry on with the assignment to different schools across the globe.

When you conceive an idea, do all it takes to birth the idea because that is where your greatness lies.

Psalm 100:5

Never Give Up Exercise

Peace endured many years of struggling and making sacrifices to enter higher education in Africa. Many in the United States have had numerous educational opportunities, been awarded grants, or received scholarships to attend higher education. Those in Lagos and other African regions have not been that fortunate. Through Peace's journey, her epiphany enlightened her to a plight that would eradicate a cultural tradition. Having a teachable spirit opened her up to unlimited strategies to free other women from mental bondage. She is on a quest to see a tangible global change. Annotate any dream or vision you gave up on and which was meant to impact the world:

_____

_____

_____

CHAPTER 5

Accepting the Call
SHIRLEY JOHNSON

*"A man's heart plans his way,
But the LORD directs his steps."*
- Proverbs 16:9

I am the strong one who always accepts the call. It seems like calls with tragedy on the other end of them just ring differently; as if the ring is telling you to brace yourself for the worst. I have taken calls that range from "I love you" to "someone's sick" to "this is goodbye." These calls came because the spirits of suicide and sickness were generational strongholds in my family.

One Uncle said, *"I just called to tell you I love you,"* but it really meant "I'm in a police standoff." Even after getting him to ask the Lord for forgiveness, it ended at 4AM with him dead, suicide by cop. I still wake up between 3-4AM. At first it was because I was battling my thoughts, but now it's because the Lord speaks to me.

I have heard *"He's behind me with a gun."* I was ministering to my Uncle, but he did not speak. When he shot his wife and then himself, it spoke volumes. It set a stage for other family members to struggle with thoughts of joining him. Praise God, they did not follow through.

"The doctor's found a lump; breast cancer" was the call from my mother. *"Your Grandmother has Alzheimer's"* was another call. Then my call came from doctors. Sickness plagued my body in a nine-year battle with a chronic cough and shortness of breath. My voice is still scratchy from having coughed up blood. Thank God that I am healed today!

I have been through this and much more, and I am still here! God used it all to prepare me for the call to ministry. I now encourage others through the things that I have overcome. I can share that the joy of the Lord is my strength, because after all that I have been through, I am STILL JOYFUL!

Proverbs 16:9

Accepting the Call Exercise

By now you have read three faith-based strategies to assist you in transitioning your mindset. In Shirley's journey, she took many calls of death, grief, suicide and sickness. She did not run from adversity but faced it head on. She activated spiritual warfare during certain incidents in her life. Your mind has to be right for the fight in the spirit realm. As well, her mind had the right to minister to every voice at the end of each call. She accepted those calls and the call into ministry. Each one of those calls was a test in her testimony today that strengthened her servant leadership attributes. Annotate any test that has not turned into a testimony:

_____

_____

_____

_____

Now, take all those items you wrote down in each exercise and pray over them. Ask God to give you a strategy to be healed and delivered from those areas in your life. Good attributes of a good leader are a teachable spirit, courage, discipline and determination. There were a few things these phenomenal overcomers had to surrender to make this mental transition - and you will too if you are serious. You must be broken so God can rebuild you.

One of the biggest mistakes I made when God was trying to shift my mindset from ministry to a business mindset was that I thought I knew what I was doing! How of you already feel you know this information and you do not need any assistance. If I just described you, your will still needs to be broken before you can move. Now, if you are open to the paradigm shift taking place in your life, study this development strategy.

BUSINESS DEVELOPMENT STRATEGY

The Six Pillars of Performance

Adapted from Clay Carr, "How to Improve Performance,"

Training and Development (July 1994).

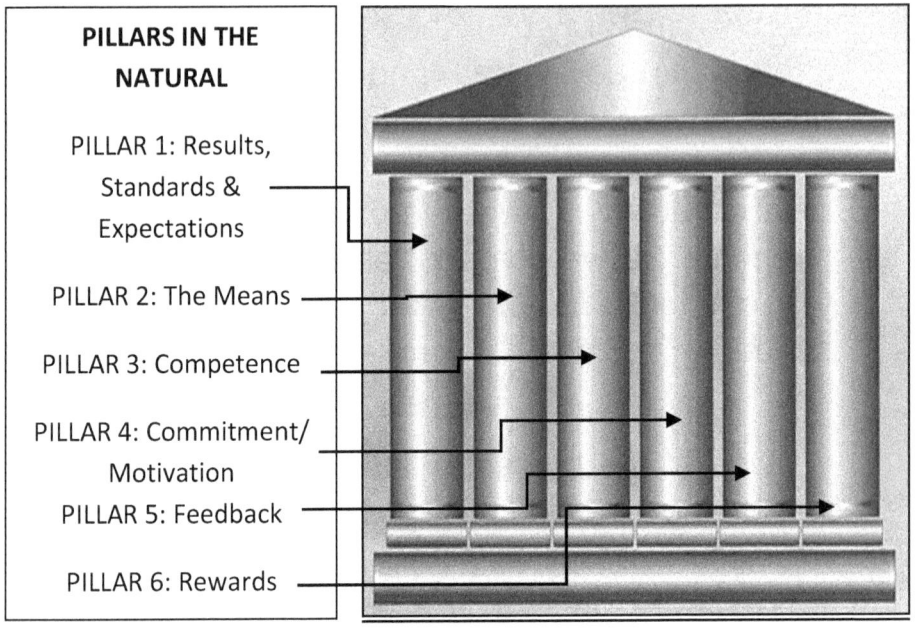

Six Pillars of Performance Spiritually

PILLAR 1: (VISION OR MISSION)

"Then the LORD answered me and said:
Write the vision
*And **make it plain** on tablets,*
That he may run who reads it.
For the vision is yet for an appointed time;
But at the end it will speak,
and it will not lie.
Though it tarries, wait for it;
Because it will surely come,
It will not tarry."
- Habakkuk 2:2

Summary: to transition your mindset, you must write the vision and make it plain. Annotate elements for your business plan, results, anticipations and expectations. It is hard to move when you do not have a clear destination or know what you are doing. Whether you are an emerging entrepreneur or you had or have a business, results and expectations are achieved through proven biblical strategies. And, even if you operate a ministry, there is still a business element you must know to be considered a legitimate ministry. Do not operate your ministry or ministry-business undercover.

Write the vision. INVEST in hiring a mentor or coach that has already achieved the goal set before you. DO NOT try to achieve your goals in the FREE99 ZONE. What is the FREE99 ZONE? Glad you asked. It is a zone where people try to harvest strategies and techniques from others without paying a cent or giving of your skills and talents FREE. This may work for a period, but it will not last. The Spirit will expose the true motive every time. However, if you are serious about transitioning from a ministry to business mindset, you must begin to think like an entrepreneur while retaining your integrity as a Christian.

I rebuke the lie of Satan that you cannot be a Kingdompreneur, obtain extra streams of income, acquire wealth, and serve God. That lie will keep you with a poverty spirit – you will be living paycheck to paycheck! It is time to come from under that spirit to create generational wealth to leave an inheritance for our children's children. And before you think it, let me say it: generational wealth is not just money.

We are supposed to be lenders, not borrowers. Well, how can you lend what you do not have? How can you have anything if you have not planned to obtain it? So, get in the face of God and write the vision He has given you. No excuses. No procrastination. No limits on investing in yourself. Do not allow your vision to end up in the graveyard.

PILLAR 2: (EQUIPMENT AND SUPPLIES)

*"Jesus said to them, "How **many loaves** do you have?"*
*And they said, "Seven and a few **little** fish.*
So He commanded the multitude to sit down on the ground,
*And **He took** the seven loaves and the fish and **gave thanks**,*
***Broke them** and **gave them** to **His disciples**;*
*And the **disciples gave** to the **multitude**."*
- Matthew 15:34-36

Stop thinking you do not have enough to do what God has given you to do. Examine the bold words for divine revelation. In paraphrasing the scripture, He asked "how much" do you have to go towards what you need Him to do for a reason. God wants you to "examine" what you already have "first" before He touches it - then He blesses it. He wants you to "see it before you see it." When He showed me that, I registered the hashtag to be an encouragement to myself and others. In this biblical strategy, God has already given us enough for the vision or mission if you maintain and manage; he will multiply. Access your tools, finances, etc. So, do not activate a word curse on it by "saying" otherwise. Only speak life to your vision or mission.

PILLAR 3: COMPETENCE (TRAINING, ABILITY AND SKILLS)

"Do you see someone skilled in their work?
They will serve before kings;
they will not serve before officials of low rank."
- Proverbs 22:29 (NIV)

Learn to utilize all your knowledge, skill, abilities and training from corporate or the private sector. When you incorporate them into your ministry mindset, God will increase you in multiple areas. Today you will understand why God had you on the difficult assignment on your job or why he put you through an unusual test. Consider each incident a Military Boot Camp, and you survived. Now, annotate all your knowledge, skills, abilities (K.S.O'S), training, or the most **minute** things you are passionate about doing. This mini-exercise will identify some of your valuable competencies to structure your business mindset around. Eventually, your skills (competencies) will place you before great and powerful kings, officials, or leaders for God's glory.

PILLAR 4: COMMITMENT / MOTIVATION

*"Let nothing be done through **selfish ambition** or conceit, but in lowliness of mind let each **esteem others** better than himself. Let each of you look out not only for his own interest, but also for the **interest of others**."*
- Philippians 2:3

In John C. Maxwell's, "The 21 Irrefutable Laws of Leadership" he states that under Law 12: The Law of Empowerment, only secure leaders give power to others. Whether you read this entire chapter or glean from the quote, your life will never be the same as a leader. A good leader knows how to follow, how to delegate, and how to sow into others for their growth. According to Maxwell, "The people's capacity to achieve is determined by their leader's ability to empower." As you transition your mindset, your vision must contain empowerment tools needed by those attached to you. Although it is your vision, if not structured purposely to include the interest of others, you may miss your target audience. So, at times, you may feel like you have "compromised" your vision or mission. When actually, your mindset is maturing to a point of resilience as you commit yourself to motivate, lift and empower others.

PILLAR 5 and 6

"A strong woman accepts both compliments and criticism graciously, knowing that it takes both sun and rain for a flower to grow."

- Author unknown

Feedback is needed in ministry or business. Leaders grow by "receiving" wisdom, ideas, critiques, or criticism from others. You may be conditioned to always doing things your way. However, as you transition from ministry to a business mindset, it is time to adapt to others point of view to propel you forward. Also, consider doing a S.W.O.T. Analysis to identify other areas in your life that might need immediate attention. Believe you me, you will see unlimited rewards down the line. Just focus on meeting the need of others and let the journey of these phenomenal overcomers to be an encouragement to you. They lifted the veil in sharing their testimony with the world. Now, you pass the torch and lift your veil to empower someone else.

Meet the Authors

Ollyn Yvonne Adkins is a native Texan, educated through Los Angeles Independent School District, and a Licensed Vocational Nurse. Having lived an unmanageable life style of domestic violence and drug addiction, she met Christ Jesus and overcame spiritual disease. With four other people, she founded Restored to Sanity Group Narcotics Anonymous Fort Worth Texas. After completing the 12 Steps, the literature states, "Having had a spiritual awakening" God revealed a plan for the still suffering addict, for those who would accept His Son Jesus. Forsaking all other gods. From this spiritual revelation, Recovery Room Ministries was birthed: a Christ-centered ministry and curriculum developed to aid in the restoration of the hurting, to a life of hope, love, deliverance, sanctification and stability. Ollyn has a heart for ministry. As an evangelist, her life's purpose is offering salvation, deliverance, and sanctification to God's people and leading them back to Christ. She can be reached at ollyn.adkins@gmail.com.

"Success isn't about how much money you make, it's about the difference you make in people's lives."

- Michelle Obama
First African-American First Lady of the United States

Shirley J. Johnson is a minister, servant leader and overcomer. She has survived struggles with identity, sickness, tragic family loss and the challenges of ministering to people while you are hurting.

She has spent over ten years leading ministries, teaching and preaching at various engagements. Her love for God is the source of her strength. She has a genuine desire to serve God's people through her ministry, STILL JOYFUL where she imparts that tragedy does not have to steal your joy.

Her background includes service in the U.S. Air Force and the Department of Homeland Security. She has a degree in Communications from Dallas Baptist University and has studied courses in

Business, Technology, the Holy Bible, Christianity, and Religion.

Preaching an uncompromising word, prayer and exhortation are all a part of her service to God. She is currently writing her first book. She can be reached at stilljoyfulministries@yahoo.com.

"Challenges make you discover things about yourself that you never really knew."

- Cicely Tyson
Legendary American Actress

Born and bred in North Carolina, and now a long-term Texan, **Loretta Howard** has a Bachelor of Science in Business Management, and she has completed some MBA classes.

She is a consultant with Legalshield where she shows singles and families how to have access to legal services at a minimum monthly cost. She truly believes that the difference between the haves and have nots is access to proper legal advice, proper legal counsel and proper legal representation if necessary.

She is in the process of starting a non-profit called Mrs. Lottie's Pantry in memory of her mother, Mrs. Lottie Smith Howard. The non-profit will help underemployed and unemployed people with food and gas.

As a never married single, she reminds other single ladies to stay dangerous by honoring God, tithing, working diligently, investing in their 401k, and keeping their money in their pocket.

Loretta is in the process of writing her first book, "The Dirt Road Blessing." She can be reached at lorettahoward823@gmail.com.

"If you don't know what your passion is, realize that one reason for your existence on earth is to find it."

- Oprah Winfrey
Media Proprietor and Philanthropist

Chukwudire Peace Uchechukwu is a seasoned nurse with more than six years of professional experience. She lives in Lagos, Nigeria. In her course of work, she discovered the need to create awareness among students in different schools on the risks and dangers of Female Genital Mutilation (FGM), and its causes in the medical and emotional being of the female child.

She is leading a campaign in conjunction with the Ministry of Health of Women Affairs and Poverty Alleviation and Ministry of Youth Development and Empowerment Lagos Nigeria against Female Genital Mutilation at Debiruss College in Lagos, Nigeria. The campaign is to be held on the 11th of October 2018.

She is working with the students at Debruises College to organize the maiden program in the above-mentioned school. Her aim is to get the students fully involved in planning and organizing campaigns against Female Genital Mutilation while she assists them during the process, thereby eradicating FGM by the next generation. She is an international speaker and was featured on Nigeria's first radio station for women.

You can connect with Peace on Instagram at uc_peace and Facebook as Peace Uche. She can be reached at alwaysalert2001@yahoo.com.

"We realize the importance of our voice when we are silenced."
- Malala Yousafzai

Visionary **Linda D. Lee** is the CEO and Founder of LL Media Group, LLC, a Personal Development Consultancy company. She is a Professional Certified Life Coach (PCLC), Certified Christian Mentor (CCM), International Speaker, Personal Development Consultant, Award-winning author, and a voice for the voiceless. She has amassed over 20 years' combined experience in personal development, customer service, and Emotion Management Strategies.

With her years of experience and wealth of revelatory knowledge, she touches lives through workshops and webinars to build healthy relationships virtually or physically, as a *Family Relationship Midwife,* ® one mindset at a time.

As a prolific writer she has been labeled a 'Powerhouse Phenomenon' by Huffington Post, and has been featured on the internationally syndicated platforms KHVN Heaven 97, The Cedric Bailey Show, LaVida News, Immerss TV, I Am Princess of Suburbia TV, *I Am A Storyteller Magazine, Queen "B" Magazine*, Access 34 TV, Anthony Chisom Conversations TV Show, Redboi Raydio Show, POD City Podcast Network, TuneIn Radio, GAB Radio, Donny "B" Gospel Show, V Inspired Show, The Ricardo Miller Show, Fishbowl Radio Network, Stellar Award Candidate 'Big Mouth' Radio Show, *Modern Citizen Magazine, Today's Purpose Woman Magazine, YOU Magazine, Divine Inspiration Magazine,* and others. Linda is the author of, *In Bed with a Snake, How to Divorce a Curse*, and *FREEDOM: Creating a Therapeutic Culture of Men. In Bed with a Snake* was the winner of the Black Essence Inc. "Excellent Book" Award and the Indie Author Legacy Award for Memoir of the Year.

Linda garnered respect and admiration as she facilitated workshops and undertook speaking engagements in Cape Coast, Ghana, Africa, and London, UK. In 2018, she facilitated the Man-Up Summit to restore the voice of men and remove the stigma regarding their communication, counseling and trauma. Additionally, she launched the inaugural Tutor Purity Ceremony to teach others how to have healthy relationships and live a life pleasing to God, in life, business or career. Next, the global Purity Movement will take place in

Mozambique, Africa with covenant sister, Dr. Lindie Sanders.

Linda and her husband, Bruce, live in the Dallas-Ft. Worth area. They have three children, seven grandchildren and two great-grandchildren. Both are licensed ministers and service the community in multiple capacities. As well, both facilitate personal development, with Bruce specializing in Trauma Informed Care and Linda with Emotional Management Strategies and Sustainability Plans.

To learn more, visit her website at
www.1lindadlee.com or linktr.ee/1lindadlee

Personal Development Tools
Available online where books are sold

Black Essence Inc. Award

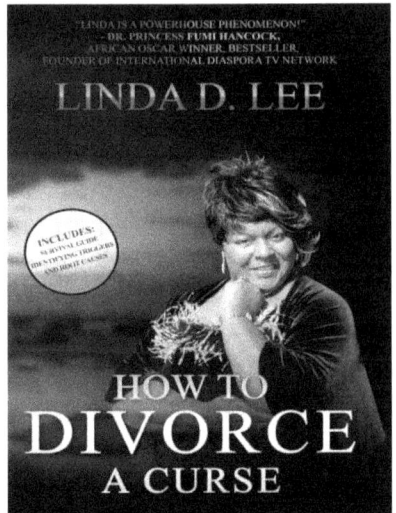

Indie Author Legacy Memoir of the Year Finalist

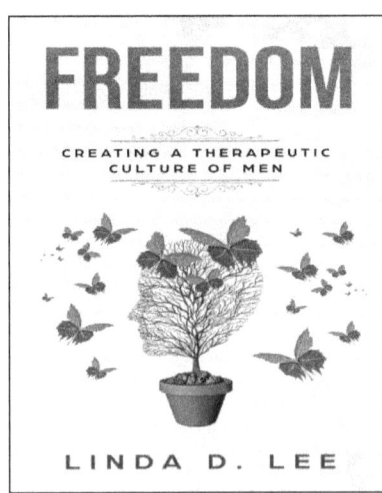

www.ingramcontent.com/pod-product-compliance
Lightning Source LLC
LaVergne TN
LVHW051205080426
835508LV00021B/2823